1 At Whitby

2 *(overleaf)* Whitby. The Market Place in front of the Tolbooth, which was built, 1788, at the expense of Nathaniel Cholmley and designed by Jonathan Pickernell, the engineer of Whitby pier

Victorian and Edwardian

YORKSHIRE

from old photographs

Introduction and commentaries by

A. B. CRAVEN

B. T. BATSFORD LTD

LONDON

B. T. Batsford Limited
4 Fitzhardinge St, London W1
Printed in Great Britain
by The Anchor Press Ltd
Tiptree, Essex

First published 1971
Reprinted 1981
ISBN 7134 0117 6

3 Scarborough. Promenaders

CONTENTS

ACKNOWLEDGMENTS

This book was only produced with the very willing help of librarians and their staffs in many Yorkshire libraries, who made available and searched out likely photographs, many of which it has not unfortunately been possible to use. The author and publishers are indebted to them. For the photographs which have been reproduced they wish to thank:

Bradford Public Library, 6, 7, 9, 51, 57, 137; *F. Frith & Co. Ltd.,* 8, 32, 33, 40; *Charles Goulding, Beverley,* 49; *Harrogate Public Library,* 34, 35, 36, 37, 93, 117, 121, 133, 135, 136, 138, 158, 159; *Huddersfield Public Library,* 10, 11, 12, 13, 14, 94; *Hull Public Library,* 65, 95, 96, 97; *Leeds Public Library,* 4, 15, 16, 17, 18, 20, 21, 23, 24, 25, 26, 55, 74, 77, 87, 106, 107, 110, 111, 115, 116, 124, 131, 139, 142, 146, 147, 149, 152, 153, 154, 160, (McKenna Collection) 102, 104, 105; *Mansell Collection,* 19, 22, 53, 54, 56; *W. H. Masterman,* 120; *Middlesbrough Public Library,* 61, 62, 63, 119, 122, 123, 128, 140, 155; *Miss Beatrice Peel,* 92; *Pontefract Public Library,* 38, 39, 112, 113, 114, 126, 132, 134; *Radio Times Picture Post Library,* 66; *Scarborough Public Library,* 3, 5, 67, 68, 69, 75, 76, 78, 79, 80, 82, 85, 86, 88, 89, 90, 125, 127, 141, 157; *Science Museum,* 41; *W. Eglon Shaw/Sutcliffe Collection,* 1, 2, 50, 58, 59, 60, 64, 71, 72, 73, 81, 83, 84, 91, 100, 101, 103, 143, 144, 145, 148, 150, 151, 156; *Sheffield Public Library,* 27, 28, 29, 30, 31, 98, 99, 118, 129, 130; *Skipton Public Library,* 52; *Victoria and Albert Museum,* 42; *York Public Library,* 43, 44, 45, 46, 47, 48, 108, 109.

The author wishes to thank also Mr J. Roberts of Farsley for information on the firm of Abram Peel & Bros.; Mr M. E. Taylor of Leeds for his work on the photographs; and Mrs A. G. Powell for typing and secretarial assistance.

4 Harewood, Mr A. B. Gill, of the staff of the City Engineers' Department, at Leeds, on his way to discuss the extension of the water mains from Eccup Reservoir, Leeds, to Harewood village, 4th August, 1899. Photograph, Nichols

INTRODUCTION

There are great contrasts and variety in Yorkshire: between coal and industry in the south and agriculture in the north; between the industrial and commercial cities and the country areas; between the Pennine uplands and the flatlands of the vales of York, Pickering and Howden; between the moorlands, the pastures and woods of the lowlands, the chalk wolds and the coast. A part of this variety is illustrated in these photographs, but not all of it.

The selection is limited first by what the Victorians thought was worth photographing. Mining and industry did not appear to fall into this category. The effect of the industrial revolution in Yorkshire, which both in mining and in the woollen industry was felt in the country areas as well as in the industrial cities and towns, is not therefore fully shown. The price paid for the country's greatness in the nineteenth century is evident here only in the cities, and then mainly in industry's by-products—the squalor and grimness of over-crowding, the stunted bodies and wretched clothes of slum children, the in-sanitary appearance of a slaughterhouse—but not in direct photographs of the interiors or exteriors of mills, factories or workshops.

The building of the railways, one of the outstanding achievements of the Victorians, is an exception and must then as now have attracted its enthusiasts and so was fairly widely photographed. So too was the building of waterworks, that other example of our continued dependence on Victorian capital investment.

What are now perhaps regarded as specifically Victorian emphases are fairly evident: the delight in pomp and ceremony, the dressing up of and for public occasions; the serious and mainly middle-class pursuits of archaeology, anti-

5   Fishing boats in South Bay

quarianism and natural history; the good causes—vegetarianism, anti-vivi-section, etc.

There is a prevalence of bands, which is not surprising in Yorkshire. There is a prevalence of children, which is also not surprising in the nineteenth century: the children of the poor in uniform in charity schools, the children of the well-to-do in uniform in private schools, and children out of school in varying degrees of well-being. On the whole women give an impression of elegance while men manage only to look as though their clothes were too thick and too infrequently cleaned.

Smaller contrasts also stand out: for example, the number of boats in Scarborough Bay compared to the scene today. Scarborough of course was the

place where the whole business of the British seaside holiday began. It was promoted as early as 1626 as a chalybeate spa by a Mrs Farrow. Medical backing followed in 1667 from Dr Wittie of Hull who not only commended the chalybeate but went one better than the rival inland spas by offering the sea—as medicinal drink and medicinal bath. From this followed Rowlandson's naked ladies in Scarborough Bay in 1813 and all the later glories of the seaside holiday, which at Scarborough during the last hundred years has increasingly overshadowed the claims of the spa. Harrogate during the nineteenth century became more of a spa than Scarborough. Now that the cure has lost favour Harrogate has turned not to holidays, but mainly to conferences to keep its hotels in business.

The selection of these photographs is also limited by what survives. Most of them are from public collections because these are more accessible. The places where photographs have been collected and survive are naturally more heavily represented in this book: many of the others are not represented at all. To offset this chance emphasis the arrangement is not entirely by place. Some of the photographs have been regarded as typical and have not therefore been duplicated: a slum courtyard in Leeds, for instance, looks much the same as its counterpart in Sheffield or Bradford.

The nineteenth century was a period of immense and rapid growth in the industrial cities of Yorkshire. The population of Leeds in 1801 was 53,162; in 1851 it was 172,023; in 1901 it was 428,572: the surprising thing was not that people were badly housed but that they were housed at all. The cities were in consequence of this growth largely Victorian, and remained so in feeling until the recent and continuing large-scale changes due to road developments, slum clearance and the use of tower blocks. The smaller country or market towns, subject to less rapid and extensive change and decay, retain more from earlier periods. The villages tend to look dusty and deserted.

There are in fact far more Victorian and Edwardian photographs available than could be used in this volume. The greatest difficulty has been in rejecting the majority.

CITIES AND TOWNS

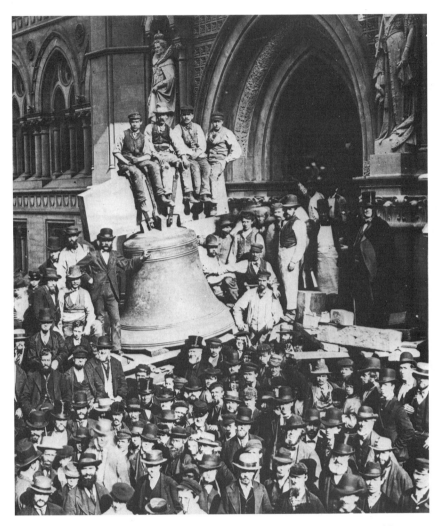

6 Bradford, the Town Hall. Opened 1873 by the Lord Mayor of Bradford, Alderman Matthew William Thompson. Architects: Lockwood and Mawson of Bradford. Has an Italianate tower which is a replica of the Palazzo Vecchio at Florence, and one of the largest peals of bells in England. The photograph is of the installation of the four-ton hour bell 'Matthew William'—supplied by Gillett and Bland, Steam Clock Factory, Croydon, and cast by J. Taylor & Co., Loughborough

7   Forster Square. In the centre background the statue of W. E. Forster of the 1870 Education Act, in the right fore-ground that of Richard Oastler of the Ten Hour Bill. The G.P.O. building was opened in 1886. Bradford Cathedral tower (1508) behind, was used as a strong point by Sir Thomas Fairfax's forces during a Royalist attack on Bradford in the Civil War

8   Darley Street

9   Town Hall Square in the 189

10 Huddersfield. View from the footpath leading to Fixby Park in 1886

12 Railway Street. The Corinthian Station built 1847–48 by J. P. Pritchett, of York is described by Sir Nikolaus Pevsner as 'one of the best early railway stations in England'

HUDDERSFIELD

11 King's Mill Bridge, Almondbury, built in 1869 to replace an old wood bridge erected in 1847 and washed away by the Holmfirth Flood in 1852

13 Westgate. Old buildings taken down in 1869 and 1870 to make way for the Bipam Buildings (1871–72) and the Byram Arcade (1880–81)

HUDDERSFIELD

14 The Market Place. The Jubilee Fountain was erected in 1887 by Sir John William Ramsden, Bart. from the design of R. W. Edis. The Waverley Hotel, built in 1880 was demolished before 1899. St Peter's Parish Church, rebuilt by J. P. Pritchett of York in 1834–36, was originally a Norman foundation

15 Upper Briggate *c.* 1860. The Corn Exchange facing down Briggate at the crossing of Upper- and Lower- head Rows was built in 1829 and pulled down in 1869

LEEDS

16 Whitehall Road Suspension Bridge. Designed by J. W. Leather and built in 1827. This was one of the first cast-iron bridges with suspension arcs instead of chains. It was replaced in 1886 by the present Monk Bridge

17   Briggate. The east side from the junction with Boar Lane. 1899

18 Lower Briggate, West side, 1867. The *Golden Fleece* Inn at the corner of Boar Lane was demolished in 1867 when Boar Lane was widened. Holy Trinity Church, the last eighteenth-century church left in Leeds, behind; designed by Halfpenny, built 1721–27; tower 1839 by Chantrell

19 Briggate in the 1890's

20 The Rose and Crown Yard off Briggate. The Queen's Arcade was built in 1888 on this site

LEEDS

21 The Rotation Office Yard, 1872–73. This yard ran from Kirkgate to Call Lane before the extensi
Duncan Street into Vicar Lane. The name is reputedly derived from the fact that a Magistrates' Court
in a room in this yard alternated its sittings with the Court held in the Moot Hall

22 General Infirmary. Gothic brick, designed by Sir George Gilbert Scott and opened in 1869. St George's Church in the background *c.* 1836–38 by John Clark: the spire was removed in 1962 because the structure was unsafe

23 Slaughter-house off Vicar Lane. One of three slaughter-houses close to Wood Street, in the late 1880's

24 Riley's Court, between Off Street and York Street, not far from the Parish Church graveyard. The L.N.E.R. line, Leeds to York, passed over the court. Demolished *c.* 1904

25 43 Reginald Terrace, approximately 1889. Gordon Stowell's novel, *The History of Button Hill*, was set in this area, beginning at about the same date. 'Retail shops and licensed premises were barred. From the outset the new suburb could not help but feel itself exclusive and superior. . . . Curtains of lace, looped back gracefully from the bay window were supplemented by more sombre hangings of green guipure with a ball fringe, which matched the mantel-cloth, the cloth on the dining table, and the curtain hung across the door to keep out draughts. Before the centre window of the bay a rampant aspidistra arose from a still more rampant aspidistra stand'

26 Commercial Buildings, City Square. Built 1826, designed by John Clark; demolished 1871 and replaced by the Gothic brick Royal Exchange, which in turn was demolished in 1964 and replaced by the tower block of the present Royal Exchange House

27 Looking down High Street from Fargate in the 1880's

SHEFFIELD

28 High Street in the 1860's. Parish Church gates in foreground

29 *(overleaf)* High Street, *c.* 1905

30   Pinstone Street, 1890. St Paul's Church in background—demolished in the 1930's

31 Family group of the 1850's. From a collodian negative by Arthur Hayball. His two brothers, John and Thomas, and their wives, with Mrs Arthur Hayball and her three daughters

32 Doncaster, St Sepulchre Gate

33 In the Valley Gardens *c.* 1906

35 *(left)* The Royal Baths, by F. T. Baggalay and F. Bristowe, 18

36 *(below)* The Royal Baths. Turkish Bath, cooling roo
Harrogate is almost entirely Victorian and Edwardian. From t
early nineteenth century it was a spa-town, developing its bat
and cures, and building its hotels until the turn of the centur
With the decline of the cure it has now become a 'conferenc
town

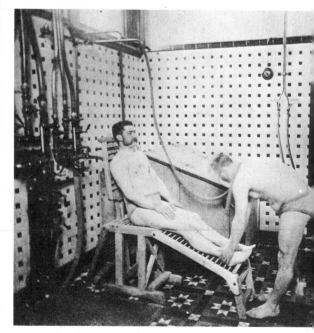

34 . The Stray, looking much less well-groomed than it now does. Montpelier Parade on the left; Cambridge Crescent in the centre; Prospect Hotel (1859, enlarged 1870) on the right

HARROGATE

37 Ripon Road looking up Parliament Street. The Royal Hall, originally the Kursaal, by R. J. Bean and F. Marcham, opened 1903 by Sir Hubert Parry, on the left

38 The Old Town Hall, built 1785, on the site of the Moot Hall which was destroyed in the Civil War, was rebuilt in 1656, and demolished to make way for the present building

PONTEFRACT

39 The Buttercross (1734) and St Giles' Church. The Church has been much altered. The north arcade is early fourteenth century, the south arcade eighteenth century, the Chancel 1869, the tower 1707 rebuilt 1793

40 Ripon, The Market Place. The Town Hall on the right was built in 1801 by James Wyatt. The Cathedral is in the distance

41 The Staythe or King's Staith, *c.* 1876. Photograph by Fox-Talbot

YORK

42 Tower, Lendal Ferry in the early 1860's

43 Lendal Ferry. The ferry operated across the River Ouse until the opening of Lendal Bridge in 1863. On the left the fifteenth-century Guildhall, reduced to a shell by bombing in 1942 and now restored

45 Pavement in the 1860's. Rowntree's original shop is the one with the bow windows

YORK

St Leonard's Place

46 The Junction of Goodramgate and Petergate looking towards the Minster

YORK

48 *(overleaf)* Lop Lane before the building of Duncombe Place in 1864

47 Fossgate

THE COUNTRY

49   Plough teams from near Beverley

50 North-east Yorkshire moors

51 East Riddlesden Hall. The central part of the Hall with the round-arched porch was built in 1648 for a Halifax clothier, James Murgatroyd. The buildings to the right of this are older

52 Eastby Village

53 Fountains Hall entrance gate, 1856. The Hall was built in 1611 by Sir Stephen Proctor

54 Fountains Abbey in 1856. East window and t

55 Huddleston Hall, Sherburn in Elmet. Horse mill for grinding corn. In general use mid-nineteenth century. Photographed *c*. 1902

56 Haworth Parsonage at the time of the Brontës. The house was built about 1800

58   *(overleaf)* North-east Yorkshire moors, Sheep dipping

57   Shipley Glen. British Temperance Tea and Coffee House

59   North-east Yorkshire moors, Ploughing

THE COAST

60 Robin Hood's Bay. The slipway. A fishing village until after the First World War Robin Hood's Bay is now entirely a holiday resort

61   View downstream from Victoria Bridge

MIDDLESBROUGH

62 Middlesbrough. The river Tees frozen over at
Christmas, 1860

63 Middlesbrough. The Erimus ferry steamer, built 1888, which crossed the Tees to Port Clarence before
the opening of the transporter bridge in 1911. Here the bridge is shown under construction

64 Victoria Pier and landing stage. The old 50-gun frigate *Southampton* was used from 1868 as a training ship for boys

HULL

65 Hull. Prince's Dock, formerly Junction Dock, opened 1829: designed by James Walker. Dock Offices built 1871. Wilberforce Monument erected 1834–35 by subscription, the work supervised by John Clark, of Leeds, architect

Redcar. Six miles of golden sands. '. . . how well Redcar is adapted to the debilitated class of invalids only by reason of its powerfully tonic atmosphere and excellent bathing but because of the natural ities afforded by its extensive beach for easy exercise and locomotion.' Dr Oliver of Redcar, 1869

67 Scarborough. North Bay and Castle

68 Scarborough. South Bay

69 Scarborough. South Shore. The Spa (1880) designed by Thomas Verity, and the Grand Hotel (1867)

70 Scarborough. Middle pier. 1900

71 *(overleaf)* Whitby

72   Whitby. The erection of the Caedmon memorial cross on the cliff near the Abbey, 1898. The cross was unveiled by the Poet Laureate, Alfred Austin

73   Whitby. Milk deliveries

74 Staithes. Watching the boats out. Staithes, once an active fishing village, is now almost entirely a holiday resort. Photograph by Godfrey Bingley

75 Bempton Cliffs. Gathering sea-birds' eggs. The men wore billy-cock hats padded with cotton wool (or tall hats) as a protection from falling stones

THE SEA

76 Scarborough. Wrecks in the South Bay: *Lily, Black Eyed Susan, Bosphorus.* 1880

77 Flamborough. Fishermen
by Godfrey Bingley

78 Sandside, 1854

80 Scarborough. The life-boat going out

82 Scarborough. Scottish girls gutting and packing herring, as they still do when the herring fleet visits Scarborough

81 Whitby. Launching the lifeboat

83 *(overleaf)* Whitby. Fishermen tarring a boat

84   Whitby. A sailing ship. Until 1870 Whitby was a ship-building and ship-owning port. This
activity declined after 1870 as steam and iron displaced sail

THE SEASIDE

85 Scarborough. Bathing machine

86   Scarborough. Minstrel show

88   Scarborough. North Shore

87   Scarborough. Minstrel show:
South Shore. Photograph by
Godfrey Bingley

89 Scarborough. Spa Band, 1894. G. W. Turner, conductor

90 Scarborough. Children paddling

INDUSTRY AND CRAFTS

91   Whitby. Jet work-shop

92 Bradford. Management and employees at Abram Peel & Bros., Ltd., worsted piece dyers of Albion Dyeworks, Dudley Hill, Bradford, taken in 1888. The guiding spirit, Squire Pool, master-dyer, third of five brothers in the partnership, is in the centre of the middle row, in dark jacket and grey cap. The eldest brother, William, is second from the right on the back row; the second brother, Mark, warehouse foreman, in traditional check smock, is on the extreme left. The fourth brother, Abram, later to found a large combing mill, is absent; the youngest, Jesse, peeps out shyly, fourth from the right on the back row. He was an accomplished dyer, of liberal views, in sharp contrast to Abram, who became a rather bigoted Primitive Methodist, insisting on chapel attendance as a condition of employment in his combing shop.

Miss Beatrice Peel, daughter of Jesse Peel, still lives in her father's house fifteen yards from the dyehouse. The firm is still operating as Robinson & Peel

93 Harrogate. J. Brown, Saddler, Chapel Street

95-7 Hull and Barnsley Railway.
The building of the Hull and Barnsley
Railway, opened 1885

98 Sheffield. Wilson's Snuff Mills, Sharrow, Sheffield. These mills have been producing snuff by water-wheel since 1745

99 Sheffield. Traveller's porter waiting in *The Moor*

100   Whitby. Building of the Whitby-Scarborough Railway, opened in 1885

101   Ruswarp. Building the railway viaduct at Ruswarp—Whitby to Scarborough line, 1885

SHOPS AND MARKETS

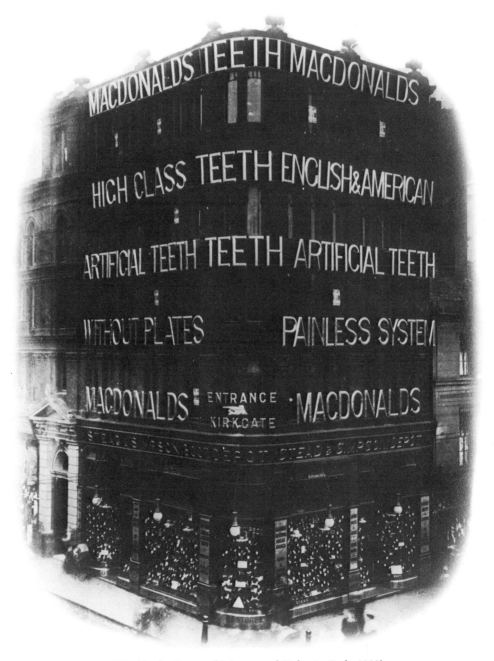

102   Leeds. Corner of Briggate and Kirkgate. Early 1900's

103   *(overleaf)* Whitby. Selling fish on the quayside

TAYLOR
THE PRACTICAL
HATTER

ESTD
1832

110 *TAYLOR* III

TAYLOR HATTER.

TAYLOR
My HATTER
FROM 123 KIRKGATE

TAYLOR HATTER.

ESTD 1832

SHAVING
SALOON

TAYLOR

ESTD 1832

CHRISTYS
SILK & FELT HATS
LONDON

PRACTICAL

EMPIRE | HAIRDRESSING | SALOON

EMPIRE | HAIRDRESSING | SALOON

EMPIRE
HAIRDRESSING
SALOON

105 Leeds. Cross Arcade. Marks and Spencer began in Leeds when Michael Marks took a stall in the open market in 1884. He moved first to the covered market, then about 1904 opened this shop

Leeds. Taylor, Hatter, 110–111 Briggate. Shortly after Joseph Taylor moved from Kirkgate to Briggate in 1901.
n, John, carried on until 1920

106   Leeds. Norton's Oyster Shop, Boar Lane, 1869

107   Leeds. Bridge End, near the junction with Water Lane

108   York. The Shambles

9   York. The market in Parliament
eet and St Sampson's Square

110 Richmond. The Market Place. The market cross is late eighteenth century. Holy Trinity church, twice in ruins and much restored, is the oldest church in the town, dating from the twelfth century: the nave is still separated by offices from the tower

VEHICLES

111 Leeds. The first overhead electric tramway in England was laid down in Leeds by the British Thomson-Houston Co., Ltd., of Rugby, from Sheepscar to Roundhay Park as an experimental track in 1891. It was extended to Kirkstall Abbey and opened for traffic in 1897

112   Pontefract. The Fire Brigade, *c.* 1897

Pontefract. Sam Hurst. Manager of Robinson
ordsworth, Liquorice Works, Pontefract, 1880

he licorice fields at Pontefract
love and I did meet,
d many a burdened licorice bush
s blooming round our feet.
                    Sir John Betjeman

Pontefract. Highways Department staff. All
s Church, *c.* 1908

115   Leeds. Rose & Co., Provision Merchants, Leeds. Horse van, between 1892–1907

Leeds. Whitehall Road
ey buses, *c.* 1910

Harrogate. Mr Yates' photo-
phic studio and miscellaneous
sport, *c.* 1890

118 Sheffield. Hunter's Bar Toll House. Pre-1884, when the toll was abolished. The collector is leaning against the corner of the house

119 Middlesbrough. The first motor car in Middlesbrough. Mr George Scoby-Smith in his $1\frac{1}{2}$ h.p. Benz. 1896

PUBLIC OCCASIONS

120 Yorkshire Yeomanry, *c.* 1897 Mr William
Masterman and Mr James Thompson

121　Harrogate. Funeral of Dr James Myrtle, Mayor of Harrogate, 1900

122   Middlesbrough. Opening of Albert Park, 1868, by Prince Arthur, Duke of Connaught

123   Middlesbrough. Albert Park, 1887: The Jubilee

124 Scarborough, *c.* 1870. Gun crews closed up around a Whitworth rifled field gun, another on a sliding carriage, and two 42 pounder smooth bores. Photograph by Nichols

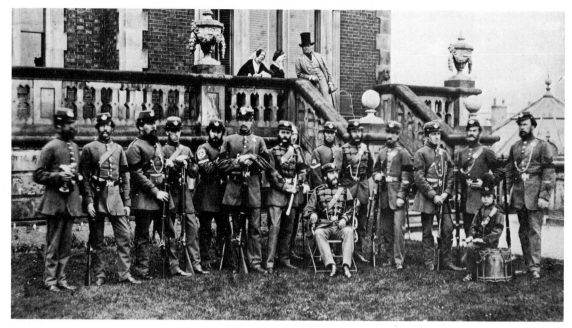

125   Scarborough. Scarborough Rifle Volunteers at St Nicholas House. 1861. The house was later purchased by the Corporation from a banker, J. W. Woodall, and in 1903 converted into the Town Hall

126   Pontefract. Roall water works. The Mayor, W. Mathers, cutting the first sod, 1888

127   Scarborough. Sir George Sitwell electioneering in July 1895—with Sir Charles Legard. The seat was won by the Liberal, J. Compton Ricketts, with a majority of 24

128   Tees Valley Water Board. Cutting the first sod at Blackton Reservoir, in Baldersdale, near Barnard Castle, 1890. The reservoir was completed in 1896

129 Sheffield. Sunday-school gathering in Norfolk Park, Whitsuntide, 1895: the famous Sheffield Whitsing, started in 1813 'like a second Pentecost' by the Sheffield Sunday School Union. From 1857 it was held in Norfolk Park, lent for these occasions by the Duke of Norfolk

130 Sheffield. Fargate, during the Queen's visit in 1897 to open the Town Hall

RECREATIONS AND CAUSES

131 Leeds Corporation Water-Works Department. Staff outing, 1892,
photographed by Nichols

132　Pontefract. Pomfret Victoria Brass Band, *c*. 1900. Known as the 'Ale and Bacca' Band

133　Harrogate. A Band outside Holroyd's Photographer's shop at the corner of Parliament Street and Chapel Street

135 Harrogate. An ox-roasting in 1887. The ox was given by Samson Fox, founder in 1874 of the Leeds Forge, who lived in Harrogate and was Mayor from 1889–92

36   Harrogate. London and Provincial Anti-Vivisection Society

137   The Grassington Antiquary: Jonathan Crowther, 1905

138   Harrogate. Tableau at the Town Hall, 1889

139 Fenay Hall, near Huddersfield. An excursion of the Leeds historical society, the Thoresby Society, 27 June 1896. The Hall is Jacobean, with internal dates 1605 and 1617. Photograph Godfrey Bingley

140 Cleveland Naturalists' Field Club outing in the 'Nineties

141 Scarborough. British Temperance League Conference, June 1872

142 Boston Spa. St Martin's (Chapel Allerton, Leeds) Picnic Club coach

143 Whitby. 'For this night only'   144 *(overleaf)* Whitby. Tennis match

145   Fyling Hall. Meet of the Staintondale Foxhounds, 1892, at that time a trencher-fed farmers' pack

146   Leeds. Headingley Cricket Ground

CHILDREN

147   Warmsworth, *c.* 1870, by Nichols

148   Whitby. 'Evicted'. 12th May 1890

149　Clapham, nr. Settle, c. 1880, by Nichols

150 Whitby. Missions to Seamen, Haggersgate House. This house in Lower Baxtergate was first rented by the Rector of Whitby and in 1892 became the property of five trustees for the Missions to Seamen

Whitby

152-3 Bridlington.
Photographs by Nichols

154 Leeds. Slum children in Bell Stre
c. 1899. This was in the Leylands, whe
the large influx of poor, immigrant Je
settled during the later part of the nir
teenth century. They came as refug
from pogroms in Russia. Many of the
found work in the tailoring industry du
ing the period when the ready-ma
clothing trade in Leeds was being ve
rapidly developed

155 Middlesbrough. Olive Street

156 Whitby School

157 Scarborough. Amicable Society School, in 1882. The society was founded by Robert North to clothe and educate the children of the poor in Scarborough. The schools were discontinued in 1893 after the establishment of the Board Schools and the income thereafter devoted to scholarships, training in handicrafts, etc

158   Harrogate College, 1891

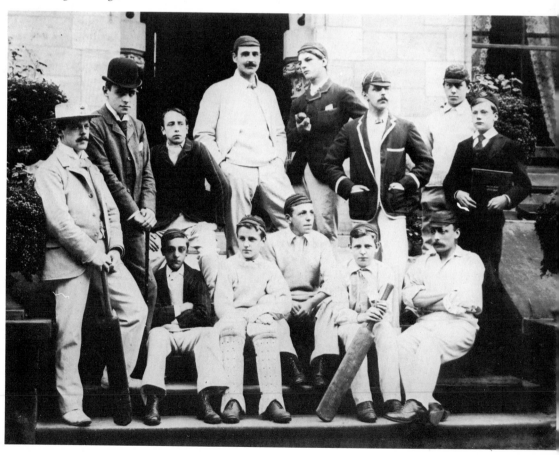

159 Harrogate. Miss Wright's school

160   Leeds. Children from a slum area